CONCEPT PAPER

Staging Point for
Project and Dissertation Proposals

FERNANDO MACOLOR CRUZ

FERNANDO MACOLOR CRUZ

MCN: C2MV9-0RG1H-Z73MV

© **copyright 2015-12-09 03:51:53** Fernando Macolor Cruz

ISBN-13: 978-1519770387

ISBN-10: 1519770383

PRINTED IN THE UNITED STATES OF AMERICA

DEDICATION

To the Almighty God,
to my mother Jean,
to all those who love the quest of knowledge
and
to all the people who continue to make a difference in this
world.

CONTENTS

ACKNOWLEDGMENTS

Acknowledgment goes to

Dr. Melinda dela Pena Bandalaria
of the University of the Philippines Open University

and

Dr. Rex Arcadio San Diego
of the Department of Education – Quezon City
(Philippines)

for all the valuable inputs.

Chapter I

THE NATURE OF CONCEPT PAPERS

What is a *concept paper?* Is it the same as a proposal paper? How is it related to a dissertation paper? Need it be defended before a panel just like the research proposal or the dissertation paper?

Indeed, these are the same questions asked again and again by first time doctoral students and project proponents alike. If one is already a doctoral student and is on his/her way to conducting his/her dissertation, s/he is expected to be well-knowledgeable about research and its processes. So asking your committee or adviser about basic research questions such as a concept paper becomes more like asking about things you admit to have missed in your prior studies!

It is becoming the standard today, that before a full research proposal be submitted, the student initially submits what is termed as a concept paper. The primary purpose for submitting one is to pave way for the collection of informal comments and suggestions coming from a panel of field experts gathered for the purpose of deliberating research concepts. Such commentaries thereby increase the chances of the full proposal's approval. This process would save the proponent valuable time, effort and resources which might have been wasted on a flawed submission that has a lower chance of acceptance and approval.

There are two entities that require a concept paper and both have different approaches.

Universities require the submission of such concept papers before a doctoral dissertation proposal is submitted. A doctoral student prepares three research concepts which s/he thinks s/he is capable of conducting.

Funding agencies have now also demanded the submission of concept papers, for basically the same practical reasons and purposes earlier stated. Most of the project concepts are presented for financial grants.

The American University of Beirut (AUB) notes that the purpose of a concept paper, from the funding agency's point of view, is to help applicants develop more competitive proposals and to save time by eliminating proposals that are not likely to be funded. The applicant's purpose in developing a concept paper is to capture the interest of the funding agency, and demonstrate that the idea they are proposing is worthy of further consideration. It further states that the first sentences of a concept paper are very important as a proponent would want the funding agency representatives or board members to continue reading.

The University of the Philippines (UP) Open University requires doctoral students to submit three concept papers that s/he must defend before a dissertation committee.

From these, Bandalaria in 2014 explained that the purpose of the topic defense is to help the student decide which of the three (3) topics presented is to be pursued, and thus provide him/her with advice from thenceforward on how to go about developing the research proposal.

Janbe.org explains that a concept paper is about the in-depth analysis regarding an intangible thought, theory, or idea. It continued to explain that it is the job of the proponent writer to inform the reader about the issue (or problem) as the audience doesn't have the knowledge about it. It explains further that if the audience has some knowledge, it is the job of the writer to add new things into the discussion.

Kenyatta University in its concept paper template states that a concept paper is meant to give one's department, college or institute an idea of the area of research interest in order to avail the necessary assistance to develop a full research proposal.

In its concept paper template, Kenyatta University advises the students to be as specific as possible in providing information.

FERNANDO MACOLOR CRUZ

Chapter 2

CHOOSING THE RIGHT TOPIC

Janbe.org explains that usually, a concept paper discusses a controversial topic which could be interpreted in various ways.

By that, a research topic needs to be something that is of great concern and interest to many and should provide valuable addition to the existing body of knowledge. The would be research topic should be something that has not been studied before, or if an initial or prior study had been conducted on the subject matter, it should either affirm, updates or revises an earlier finding. It must be something that addresses a social issue, an environmental concern, an in-depth study about culture, about science, and all other fields of human endeavor and understanding. Research topics vary from across the many disciplines and fields of knowledge.

The proposed study topic can be an attempt to test an existing theoretical proposition, or as a way of formulating a new theoretical proposition, or as an investigation of certain observed phenomena yet totally still undefined or yet not understood.

The right topic, when approved by the panel, should constitute the ability to contribute new findings. The study needs to be feasible, testable, within approved budgets, does not replicate an existing study on the same subject and should still hold value even after the study was conducted.

Most importantly, the researcher must be genuinely interested in the concepts he or she is proposing to the panel and must demonstrate his/her strong position.

Eventually, the agency or academic panel guides the proponent to the most appropriate study topic where there is the greatest value of success in terms of the quality and importance of the knowledge it will generate, the feasibility of conducting it, the genuine interest of the proponent in implementing it, and the relatedness of the chosen topic to the thrust of the college department or funding agency.

Chapter 3

PROJECT CONCEPT PAPERS

There is really no consensus as to what constitutes a concept paper and what shall not be included. Each institution or agency however can be particular about certain facts that they are after of hearing from the proponent.

The main difference between a project concept paper and an academic concept paper is the purpose for which the paper is written for. Project concept papers are written for purposes of funding while academic concept papers are written for purposes of winning the approval of the academic dissertation committee.

Difference in purpose also renders difference in their essential parts. Project concept papers typically have the following format:

I. Introduction

II. Purpose

III. Project Description

IV. Goals and Objectives/Research Questions

V. Methodology and Timelines

VI. Benefits/Anticipated Outcomes

VII. Support Needed & Costs

VIII. Contact Information

AUB explains that the first part, *Introduction*, should include some information about the funding agency. In this information, the proponent must be able to show that he has the knowledge about the mission of the funding agency and the types of projects that they support. The proponent also needs to illustrate how his own agency and that of the funding agency are intertwined in the proposed project. The proponent must be able to acknowledge the important role that the funding or sponsoring organization plays. Any other potential partners must also be included in this portion.

As a matter of introduction, not only should the proponent introduce his/her project, it is also imperative and courteous to make introduction of the proponent's organization, who they are, what they do, how long have they been in the field and other relevant information that might help establish their credibility and gain the trust and confidence of the funding agency.

AUB suggests that this should be followed by discussing questions, problems or needs that need to be addressed. This stage is briefly documenting the importance of addressing this question, problem or need. AUB also advises the use of figures or statistical data as they are very convincing in proving a point. The purpose must stress the involvement of all concerned and what has already been accomplished relative to the project. AUB cautions never to claim that the project is solely his or her own as "even the most brilliant and innovative concepts are based on the previous work of others from related fields."

Part III is Project Description. AUB states that the following guide questions should be answered: What (does) your agency plans to do? Why is this a unique approach? Who will benefit from the project? It will also be desirable for funding agencies to know how you intend to solve the problem.

Part IV should contain the basic goals and objectives or research questions. Accordingly, a goal is statement describing a broad or abstract intent, state or condition. An objective is a statement of measurable outcomes that relate to the goal. An objective includes "who, what, and when" information. It is not a statement about "how".

Any evaluation procedures to determine whether the objectives have been achieved must be included in this portion.

Next part, the methodology, should illustrate how the project will be conducted. All the techniques, approaches and processes involved must be briefly described here. A workplan or a timeline can be helpful.

It is also helpful to discuss the proponent's assessment and analysis of all previous methodologies used and applied in the main problem of the proposed program and the progress that previous efforts have made, including its failures that lead to the current need being proposed.

Inclusion of timelines will demonstrate how long it will take to finish the product or come-up with the service. If the proposed project is project management itself, how long will the project be managed. Timeline must be realistic and efficient. Time component can also be illustrated using a workplan.

Methodology is followed by benefits and anticipated outcomes. What knowledge will be generated and its usefulness must be tackled here. Who benefits must also be stated. Timeliness after the conduct of research must also be considered.

Providence College state that *Support Needed &* *Costs* portion should state the total dollar amount and general idea of type of support needed although at this stage, a detailed budget plan is not required and in some circumstances this section might be left out all together. But if one has to discuss the list of materials and resources needed to create a new product, or enumerate the type of personnel needed to provide services, it is under this section that it should be discussed as it can demonstate one's ability to grasp the needs of the project and his readiness to come-up with something.

Of course, contact information deals with the name, address, e-mail, telephone and website of the proponent.

It is best that the concept paper be brief, concise, and clear and would not exceed five (5) pages. The tone of certainty must be matched by confidence by the proponent. The planning stage shouldn't be included in the proposal, therefore no funding should be requested for such. A proponent may end the concept paper by summing-up the clearly anticipated outcomes. A short sentence that assures the funding agency that granting the proponent the chance to execute the proposed program will connect the identified gap in knowledge or service and will therefore solve the identified problem.

Aside from the parts earlier listed, some funding agencies like the Gerber Foundation demands the following additional parts or contents:

a. A Cover Letter written by a senior officer of the applying organization or from the department chair to which the principal investigator is assigned, that includes a brief introduction to the investigator(s), the goals of their research, and why they believe the project is a fit with the foundation.

b. The Number, type and age range of subjects to be studied

c. The hypothesis(es) to be tested.

d. Impact that describes how results will be beneficial

If a proponent is inclined to sending out a lot of concepts to different funding agencies, it highly recommended that s/he maintain a basic template of a concept paper where alterations, additions and changes can be readily made as most funding agencies have established guidelines on how to write the concept paper that they may consider for funding.

Chapter 4

DISSERTATION CONCEPT PAPERS

The University of South Florida College of Education describes what a concept paper is in its Advanced Graduate Handbook as a 2-3 pages presentation that will serve as an early communication device between the candidate and the Doctoral Committee about the proposed research.

On the other hand, Kenyatta University includes in its template the following as the basic parts to an academic concept paper:

I. Title of Proposed Study

II. Area of Study

III. Background to the Study

IV. Statement of the Problem

III. Objectives of the Study

IV. Questions and/or Hypotheses

V. Literature Review

VI. Theoretical Framework

VII. Proposed Research Design,

    Methods/Procedures

VIII. Bibliography

The *Title of the Proposed Study* constitutes the problem or phenomenon to be investigated. As it should be expected, the title must be short, concise and definitive of the problem to be tackled.

Area of study must indicate the specific area within the broad field of knowledge where the proposed study is mostly aligned with.

Background of the Study tells of the origins of the proposed research. It must discuss the circumstances or facts surrounding a phenomenon. It must state what the researcher had read that had an impact on him/her thinking about the topic which led the researcher to his/her current proposal.

Statement of the Problem tackles what gap in knowledge there is. It must be able to explain why the conceptualized research needs to be conducted.

Objectives of the Study simply states what the study hopes to achieve. Of course, the objectives must be perfectly aligned with the gap in knowledge and how that gap is to be filled.

Questions and/or *Hypotheses* are set of interrogative sentences that operationalize the research objectives. Here, the unknown/s are stated in question form. On the other hand, *Hypothesis* is a testable assumption about the study which is best presented or stated in null form rendering it easier to prove or disprove.

Literature Review includes all the literature

intended to be reviewed. It must also include the relevance of these literature to the study. They must be chosen carefully from the heap of information available today in printed and online formats. The review of literature may include both review of related printed materials and review of related studies conducted earlier on the topic. The review of literature must be able to present a clear framework of the study.

Theoretical Framework discusses the theory/ies that will be used in analyzing all materials. The use of such theory must also be defended and justified right at the concept stage as they are very crucial in the study. A research conducted within the wrong framework will be of no use or value.

Proposed Research Design, Methods/ Procedures refers to any of the generally accepted traditions of research. The traditions of research are the lens from where the researcher looks at the entire study. Such a tradition will spell how the study will be conducted. For example, if the study will be looked at from the tradition (lens) of culture, cultural analysis and historical analysis might be employed as research methodologies.

Bibliography includes all bibliographic citations used for reference purposes and may include all printed sources, online sources and personal communication.

For the UP Open University for example wanted hear from a doctoral students three (3) topics which are of interest to the researcher. Implied in this is the fact that the student is ready to undertake any of the topics that he will be presenting upon the approval by the student's dissertation committee. There is also the assumption that the student have read the literature related to the three (3) topics presented and can fully discuss the rationale, the research problem and the research objectives for each topic to be presented.

On academic terms, this refers to the supposed connection between and among the curricular program the student is enrolled in, the research thrust of the department and the usefulness to the student of the research topic he wishes to pursue.

Developing Research Questions

In order for a researcher to formulate clear and coherent research questions and objectives, it must first be developed from an *idea*. This idea is converted into a *single general focus question*. The general focus question will then be dissected into what we call in undergraduate research as specific questions or research questions in graduate studies. These questions must be carefully crafted to correspond to and fulfill the specific research objectives.

For example, the researcher has an idea on Disaster Communication. From there, he might develop a general focus question: How Does the Adoption of Certain Provisions in the National Disaster Management Information and Communication System of India Bring Improvement in Disaster Preparedness and Response for the Philippines in Addressing Supertyphoons?

Always remember that basing from the general focus question, what the researcher wants to achieve are listed as the objectives of the research, and the way to attain those objectives are asked as the research questions.

Research Methodology and Theoretical Framework

For dissertation concept papers, the research methodology or theoretical framework is a part which is often left vaguely discussed or inadequately tackled. This vague discussion or inadequate articulation is brought about by lack of understanding or inadequate background on research methodologies, traditions of research or theoretical familiarization. This part of the concept paper promptly identifies where the planned research rests or is situated in.

This part of the concept paper must be well stated enough for the panel members to have a clear understanding of the premises the conceptualized study is based on and directions the conceptualized study is heading.

Stating the research methodologies and theory/ies that will be employed shall clearly present the path that the planned research shall undertake. As one has a peculiar way of looking at things that has a bearing on how he sees his studies, having clearly defined methodologies and theoretical premises would guide the researcher not to switch between the many point of views in seeing things.

Generally, methodology is any of the generally accepted means or ways in conducting a study. It must be able to state how data should be gathered, including the approaches, techniques and processes in gathering such data.

Theoretical framework on the other hand, refers to the theoretical premise which one plans to employ in the study specifically for purposes of analyzing the material. One must be able to explain well fully what necessitates the use of such theory and how it was the most precise theory for that matter.

Aspiring novice or amateur researchers must be well aware of that the range of theories available now in the different branches of knowledge are generally clustered according to the original traditions they originated from. These traditions serve as ways for looking at things. For example, if one has to investigate a certain phenomenon, the question here will be, from what perspective shall you investigate the phenomenon? If it's a cultural analysis, then one most appropriately shall conduct the study from the lens of culture. If it's an empirical research, the lens the research shall be based on experience as measured through the use of the scientific methods.

Always try to provide the required information or answer each question in the concept paper (if it's in a template form). Explain the needed parts of the concept paper in a short but concise manner. The concept paper is not the full proposal, much more the final manuscript. It is simply like a fact sheet on what you wish to conduct, how do you wish to conduct it, why you wish to conduct it, and other relevant information to be presented for approval upon verification of its viability, feasibility, relevance and importance.

Lastly, the word of advice deals with beating deadlines. Funding agencies maintain grants available within specific timeframes or cycles. So be aware of the timeliness of all submissions.

Defending your Topic

Usually, the panel requires the proponent to submit three concepts and shall interview the proponent to explain each and discuss the importance and relevance of each concept. The panel expects you to be well versed of the concepts you are proposing. You will be given ample amount of time to defend each of the concepts and you are expected to be able to articulate the merits of each proposed topic.

Never assume that the panel shall grasp all the unstated ideas you failed to mention. An outline of what you are to discuss is advisable then, or better yet, a copy of all the concept papers being presented. Practice your delivery and you must be able to explain all vague terminologies that you might be forced to mention out of necessity.

The defense day will spell the success or rejection of your proposed concepts. Readying for this day and successfully defending a zeroed-in concept shall mean savings in terms of time and effort. Total rejection of the three proposed concepts implies that you have to start from scratch if you will propose another batch of concepts.

Defense these days can be conducted either face to face with the panel, or be online as technology allows it these days with media such as Skype. But in cases of online defense, a reliable internet connection must be secured, coupled with a well charged computer unit or power back-up.

Topic defense should not be an intimidating experience but shall rather be viewed as a rewarding experience as it will be your window as to how the process is conducted in preparation for the anticipated actual proposal defense or even final defense. At this stage, it will be an opportunity to improve the existing proposals or be rewarded to have an approved proposal as these experts guide you towards what you wanted to achieve.

One must remember that the defense experience of another is totally different from the experience you are about to have. Different organizations and academic institutions have different established ways of doing things. So, the best advice to a proponent here will be to be prepared for any and all eventuality. A panel member might ask you a question which you think might totally be unrelated to the proposed concepts. To you it might be surprising or even be intimidating, but you have to trust the panel members as they are the experts and one must be receptive always to the point any panel member might be driving at. Remember that your readiness to answer any question, the in-depth knowledge you have about your proposed concepts and the relevance of your proposed concepts should be well-balanced in order to have the winning concept proposal.

FERNANDO MACOLOR CRUZ

Chapter 5

SEEKING EXPERT OPINION

It would be wise to ask for the opinion of others. But such opinions must be professional in nature, meaning it has to come from authorities or experts in the field. Nothing is more valuable than a counsel given by those who have prior or existing knowledge and experience about the topic or problem.

Seeking advice from others may start right from the choice of topic. One may already have an existing knowledge about a certain idea, but may not know how to go about it. A second or third, or even fourth opinion would give the researcher a broader perspective of the idea, topic or problem being considered based on the expert's professional and time tested experiences and know-how.

Information from experts varies in scope depending upon their field of expertise or exposure to the idea or topic on the table. It may range from advice on institutional cultures, professional protocols and processes, recommendations, guidance, etc. This may include advices of professional to unconventionally practical nature. A word of advice on practical methods: there is nothing wrong in getting the job done fast and efficient as long as it is within the bounds of ethical practices and moral decency.

Expert opinion may particularly be useful especially in the methodologies or theoretical aspect. The domain of theoretical propositions abounds with so many interrelated testable assumptions. A novice may certainly get lost in the web of these deeply entrenched entanglements. A sound opinion or advice on these matters will be highly critical in the successful presentation of methodology/ies and theoretical premises of the proposed research concept.

Dalal and Bonifacio (2010) taxomomized advice (opinion) into four classifications:

- Recommending a particular course of action
- Recommending *against* a particular course of action
- Providing additional information about a particular course of action without explicitly prescribing or proscribing that course of action
- Recommending *how* to go about making the decision

In research terms, a doctoral candidate may be wanting to seek the services of a methodological adviser – an expert adviser on research methodologies. If the researcher commissions an independent adviser, he will most probably pay for his/her services. The researcher may invite the methodological adviser to be a part of the research and culminate such partnership into co-authorship of findings.

Some of the related concerns that the researcher may refer to the methodological adviser are the following:

a. Guidance to researcher as to what he really wants to accomplish.

    1. reformulation of research questions
    2. re-statement of the research objectives
    3. formulation of the research hypothesis (es)

b. Advisory on measurement instruments
c. Advisory on research design
d. Advisory on data analysis and interpretation
c. Advisory on research writing and publication of results.

Hand in hand, the researcher who knows about his craft in the field of his expertise, together with the methodological adviser who knows about methods and processes of research, can achieve better studies and obtain more accurate research results and findings.

So, it will be wise indeed to make sure that all inputs from the experts are noted and evaluated for consideration. At the end of the day, it will be the researcher who will decide how s/he will go about his/her concept proposal.

FERNANDO MACOLOR CRUZ

Chapter 6

READ, READ and READ

Just as experts and methodological advisers would generate additional oral information to the body of knowledge that the researcher may already have on his idea, topic or problem, reading from printed and online sources on the other hand would generate additional information.

Reading helps the proponent to have the widest background knowledge about his research interest. It gives him a better understanding on what he wants to do. It equips him with all the relevant information needed during the concept paper defense should the dissertation committee members ask for it.

There are two kinds of reading, one for leisure or entertainment where you tend to forget a huge chunk of information after going through the materials, and there is reading to understand intended to retain valuable information needed for some purpose or application. As we cannot always remember all salient points and important bits of information, it is necessary to take note of such important information. Notes become one's reference that is readily available for future analysis of the research concept being formulated.

Reading is imperative when conducting a research. In fact, it is so important that it has to commence even before the research proper starts. One may utilize the resources found in libraries or the internet for reading purposes. Oftentimes, on top of looking for related information to one's research, there will be an overload of information and the student would be busy sorting out which ones are useful and relevant and which ones are not. By sorting, it includes the process of classifying the kinds of information and determining where and when will they be needed in the research.

Always check about the validity of the information's source. The internet, most especially, has become a dumping ground of so much trash information that has no place in the scientific world. By scientific, only those information that had been highly tested or well-researched becomes acceptable.

For example, some circles will not honor the information contained in websites offering user-generated content such as Wikipedia. However, others do, having knowledge of the battery of very strict editors that Wiki have.

As one can see, agencies and universities alike have different treatment of available information on the internet. The same holds true even with printed materials as they hail from different publications with varying reputations.

So, the bottom line is to choose materials from reputable publications. Yet, no amount of material and information can suffice a concept or proposal paper bearing short but concise with complete information that is neatly compiled and presented to the target reader - evaluators.

Always make sure that the materials for inclusion shall be the best there is and enough as it should be.

Journals are among the best there is to delve for information as they are might be peer-reviewed which adds validity in its entries or articles. The latest researches are always favored against the older and obsolete information and findings.

In arriving to present all related literature and studies, remember to present them in a coherent manner as well. It is like composing a novel from patches of valid information, one leading to another. The resulting piece must become a masterpiece that should impress even the harshest judges.

Finally, each of the books, websites and person who engaged in a communication contributory to the research work must be recorded in the form of a bibliographic citation that will absolutely be required later on.

FERNANDO MACOLOR CRUZ

Chapter 7

AGAIN, WRITING FOR WHOM? And WHY?

$\mathbf{A}$long the course of writing the concept paper, the researcher must from time to time, recall this reference question: For whom am I writing this paper? And Why?

Remember that a proponent or student is writing not to impress nor garner acclaim for his/work, but for the sole purpose of objectively presenting a concept that s/he wanted an approval.

Remember that each agency or university has a research thrust that needs proposals to be aligned with, and that the concept paper is being written for submission that when approved might lead towards the development of a full proposal.

Tuffs University classifies proposals into the following types and funding requests:

a. *Solicited Proposal.* This type of proposal is being submitted to the funding agency as per its own request. The purpose of this might be for the conduct of a specified research or training. Invitations are handed out to experienced researchers whom the funding agency thinks they can well work with.

b. *Unsolicited Proposal.* This kind of proposal is being submitted to the funding agency in response to its research thrust but is submitted on a researcher's own volition. It may be so because the researcher found the idea or topic interesting to him/her. Unsolicited proposals are welcome to grant institutions as well as some government agencies.

c. *Pre-Proposals.* A kind of submission required by funding organization. Some would only require a technical piece with a bottom line costs while others could require cost sharing, have pre-agreed terms and conditions and administrative and science sections. There are also those that are just about as complicated as a full proposal. This is synonymous to what a *concept paper* is. Funding agencies wanted to have a peek on what the researcher intends to do, according to the agency's available funding options.

d. *Renewals.* A competing request for additional funding for an existing project whose period of performance is about to end. It generally include new work but one that is based on the results of the existing grant. They are usually peer reviewed.

e. *Resubmission.* As its name implies, a resubmission is a proposal which is revised according to critical comments it earlier received, and is being resubmitted to the sponsor agency for funding. Usually, just one resubmission is allowed. However, some agencies allows more than one resubmissions.

f. *Revision.* Revisions are requests for additional funding support for an already existing project. This is done for either of two reasons: project scope or research protocol's expansion or an unanticipated expense.

g. *Continuation.* This is a non-competing proposal requesting for additional funding and is not subject to peer review. If proposal is accepted, funding may become awarded in any of the following so called *sponsored research vehicles* or instruments:

1. *Contract.* An instrument for supporting any activity that performs a specific service or any activity that will yield a particular end or product for the government.

2. *Grant.* An instrument for providing support for an activity initiated by the proponent. The activity must fall within the guidelines and priorities of the funding agency.

The Office of Research Administration, Tuffs University, noted the following difference between a contract and a grant:

1. Contracts are used by the government to procure specific services or products from which they will derive some benefit;

2. It is the agency who establishes project specifications and therefore exercises more direction over the work than the investigator;

3. Contracts are more likely to include some "strings" attached to funding. Examples include

some tangible economic return, some degree of control over patent rights, confidentiality, or publication.

4. Grants support research whose end goal is increasing knowledge and understanding over a given subject.

h. Cooperative agreement. This is an agreement for an research or a training project jointly administered by the funding agency and the recipient institution.

i. *Sponsored Research Agreements.* These are collaborative efforts with industry partners to further develop basic research discoveries. The research agreement promptly protects the university's interests, particularly rights of publication and intellectual property ownership with the contract ensuring properly reflected the aims of the research and the policies of the university.

REFERENCES

PERSONAL COMMUNICATION:

Bandalaria, Melinda DP, Personal Comm. 3/15/14

PRINTED MATERIALS

Dalal, R. S., & Bonaccio, S. What types of advice do decision-makers prefer? *Organizational Behavior and Human Decision Processes, 112,* 11-23. 2010

UPOU Doctor of Communication Program Guidelines on The Conduct of Dissertation, UPOU, Los Banos, Laguna, Philippines.

Derr, J.. Having an impact in a multi-disciplinary setting. In H. J. Adèr & G. . Mellenbergh (Eds.), *Proceedings of the 2007 KNAW colloquium Advising on research methods:* pp. 11-20. (2008)

ONLINE SOURCES

http://janbe.org/a-perfect-college-guide-for-writing-concept-papers.html

http://viceprovost.tufts.edu/researchadmin/write-and-submit-proposal/types-of-proposals-and-funding-agreements/

http://www.aub.edu.lb/ogc/Documents/proposal/Writing_Concept_Paper.pdf

http://www.coedu.usf.edu/main/gradhandbook/advhand
book/Adv_Dissert_Proposal.html
https://www.google.com.ph/url?sa=t&rct=j&q=&esrc=s
&source=web&cd=1&cad=rja&uact=8&ved=0ahUKEwij
iIGsosvJAhVBTJQKHY_QDJMQFggaMAA&url=https
%3A%2F%2Fwww.griffith.edu.au%2F__data%2Fassets%
2Fpdf_file%2F0008%2F199619%2FDissertation-
Handbook_Version-
2012_2.0.Jan2013.pdf&usg=AFQjCNHJPbGuUcbs_b4H
H2DUnSSFne1amA&sig2=3P-
PCMzKmVgH2CeuEyOy2w

http://www.gerberfoundation.org/pd-research/research-
awards/concept-paper-format

http://www.ifrc.org/docs/idrl/919EN.pdf

http://www.ku.ac.ke/schools/graduate/images/stories/d
ocs/concept_paper_template_postgrad_students.pdf

http://www.providence.edu/academic-affairs/sponsored-
research-and-programs/Pages/Concept-Paper-
Template.aspx

http://www.wikihow.com/Write-a-Concept-Paper

ABOUT THE AUTHOR

His Royal Highness Datu Dr. Fernando Macolor Cruz, KR, AB, MPS-DC, DIA (h.c.), DES (h.c.) a.k.a. Datu (Prince) Pinadu – Cabaylo II of the Tagbanua and Cuyonon tribes is a permanent university instructor at the Palawan State University. He is also a published poet, book editor, and founder of the International Stateless Persons Organisation which assists stateless people everywhere.

He lives in Coron, Palawan, Philippines.